Jack —

God has gifted you with such an amazing family! Their love for you is only a hint of what's in God's storehouse for you!

Aloha agape & shalom
Ben Joy

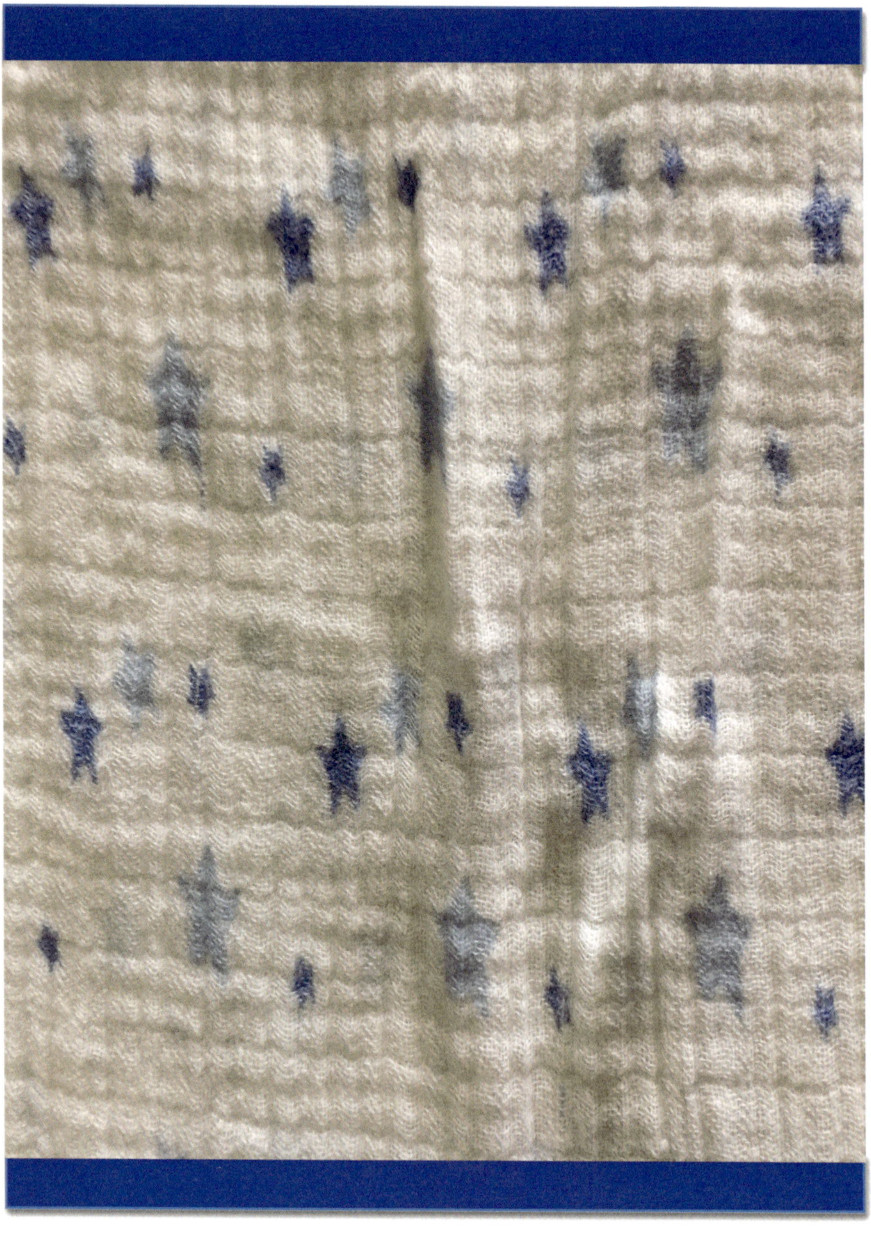

I am God's Masterpiece

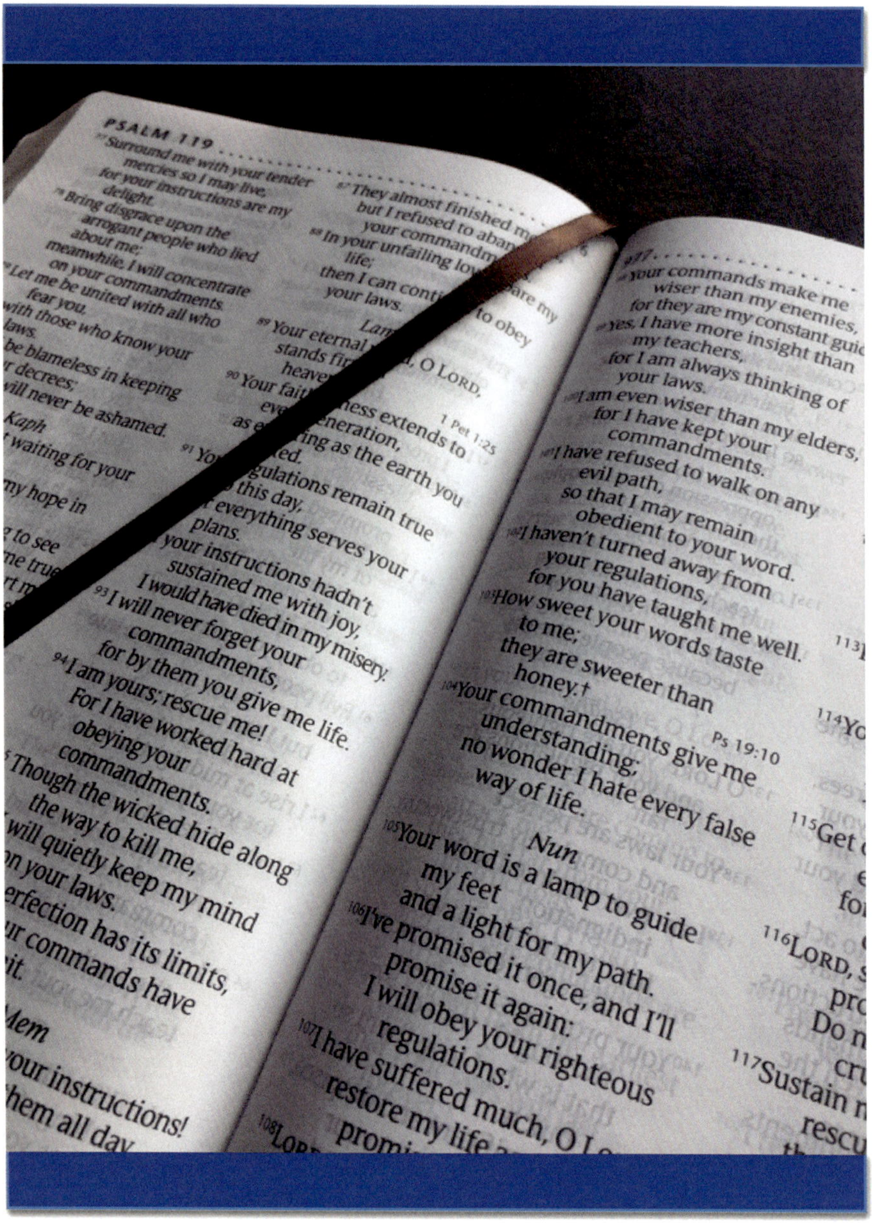
PSALM 119
Surround me with your tender mercies so I may live, for your instructions are my delight.
Bring disgrace upon the arrogant people who lied about me; meanwhile, I will concentrate on your commandments.
Let me be united with all who fear you, with those who know your laws.
They almost finished me
but I refused to aban
your commandm
In your unfailing lov
life;
then I can cont
your laws.
Your eternal
stands fir
O LORD,
ness extends to
eneration,
ing as the earth you
1 Pet 1:25
gulations remain true
this day,
everything serves your
plans.
your instructions hadn't
sustained me with joy,
I would have died in my misery.
93 I will never forget your commandments,
for by them you give me life.
94 I am yours; rescue me!
For I have worked hard at obeying your commandments.
Though the wicked hide along the way to kill me,
Your commands make me wiser than my enemies,
for they are my constant guid
Yes, I have more insight than my teachers,
for I am always thinking of your laws.
I am even wiser than my elders,
for I have kept your commandments.
I have refused to walk on any evil path,
so that I may remain obedient to your word.
I haven't turned away from your regulations,
for you have taught me well.
How sweet your words taste to me;
they are sweeter than honey.†
104 Your commandments give me understanding;
no wonder I hate every false way of life.
Ps 19:10
Nun
105 Your word is a lamp to guide my feet
and a light for my path.
106 I've promised it once, and I'll promise it again:
I will obey your righteous regulations.
107 I have suffered much, O L
restore my life
113
114 Yo
115 Get
116 LORD,
117 Sustain

Gospel for All

Written by
Bea Joy

Illustrated by
Alena Karabach

Copyright © Bea Joy

All rights reserved. No part of this publication may be reproduced, distributed, or transmitted in any form or by any means, including photocopying, recording, or other electronic or mechanical methods, without the prior written permission of the publisher, except in the case of brief quotations embodied in reviews and certain other non-commercial uses permitted by copyright law.

Illustrated by Alena Karabach

ISBN: 978-1-7324426-5-8

TO GOD BE THE GLORY!

We were brought into this world
for a purpose – to love God, and
to love each other.

God said it was up to each person
to be loving or not.
This is called free will.

Some people and even some of God's heavenly angels chose <u>not</u> to love God. Their leader is named Satan and we call them the enemy.

But God loves us and wants us in His family.
He knew we needed help to remember His great
love for us. So He sent His Son Jesus to help us.

Jesus taught people to be kind and take care of each other. Believing in Him will show us the way to Heaven.

Jesus taught that it's best to forgive each other when we make mistakes. Living this way pleases God and makes us happy and filled with joy!

Alas, the enemy doesn't like happy people.
He convinced some people to <u>not</u> like Jesus.
Those mean people chose to kill Jesus.
When Jesus went away all the people were sad.

But God is so powerful He raised Jesus from the dead and took Him back to Heaven!

Then God sent the Holy Spirit to fill their sad hearts back up with faith, hope, and love. Having this joyful heart reminds us that God wants to love us forever!

When we use our free will to love God, love each other, and believe in Jesus – then one day God will take us to Heaven to be with Jesus and all happy people!

YAY! GOD IS LOVE!

My Special Page

Scriptural References

		Romans 11:36		
		Isaiah 63:17		
		Jude 1:25		
		Ephe 2:10		
		Matt 18:12-14		
		Luke 15:4-7		
		Matt 22:37		
John 13:34	John 5:24	John 6:29	1 John 4:16	Matt 28:18
Acts 4:12	John 13:36	John 13:34-35	John 6:47	Mark 16:15
Phil 3:20	2 Peter 3:9	Genesis 2:17	Num 6:24-26	Luke 24:47
John 14:2	1 John 4:8	Deut 30:19-20	Luke 21:28	John 4:23
		Isaiah14:12-14		
		1 Peter 5:8		
		Matt 7:15		
		Isaiah 9:6		
		Luke 2		
		John 3:16		
		Matt 7:12		
		Ephe 4:32		
		John 14:6		
		Luke 11:4		
		Matt 18:21-22		
		Col 3:13		
		Matt 26:3-4		
		Luke 18:31-33		
		Matt 28:5-6		
		Luke 24		
		John 14:15-16		
		1 Cor 13:13		
		1 Cor 15:1-4		
		Luke 6:35		

Scripture quotations are taken from the Holy Bible, New Living Translation, copyright © 1996, 2004, 2015 by Tyndale House Foundation. Used by Permission of Tyndale House Publishers, Inc., Carol Stream, Illinois 60188. All rights reserved.

Scriptural Prayers

Our Father in Heaven,
Hallowed be Your name.
Your kingdom come,
Your will be done
On earth as it is in Heaven.
Give us this day our daily bread.
And forgive us our debts,
As we forgive our debtors.
And do not lead us into temptation,
But deliver us from the evil one.

May the LORD bless you and protect you.
May the LORD smile on you
and be gracious to you.
May the LORD show you His favor
and grant you His peace.

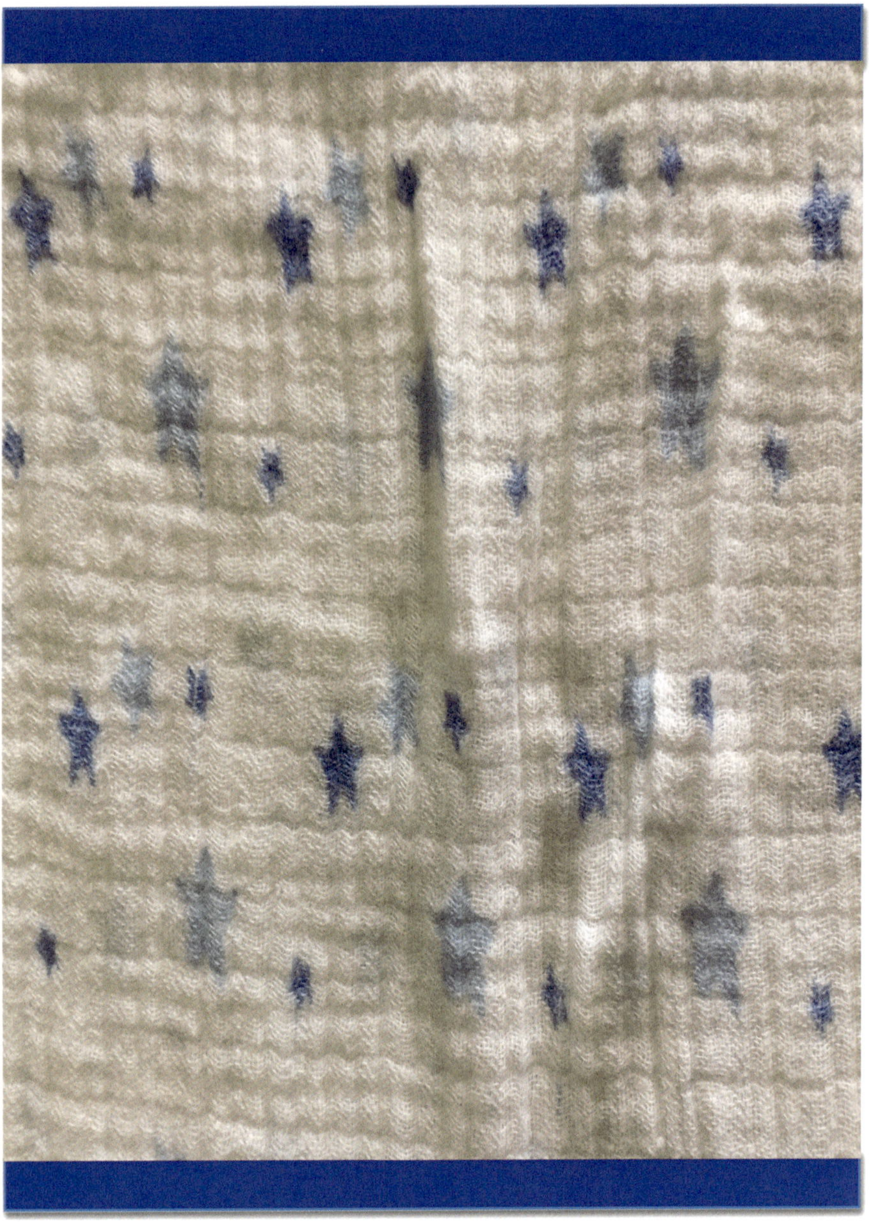

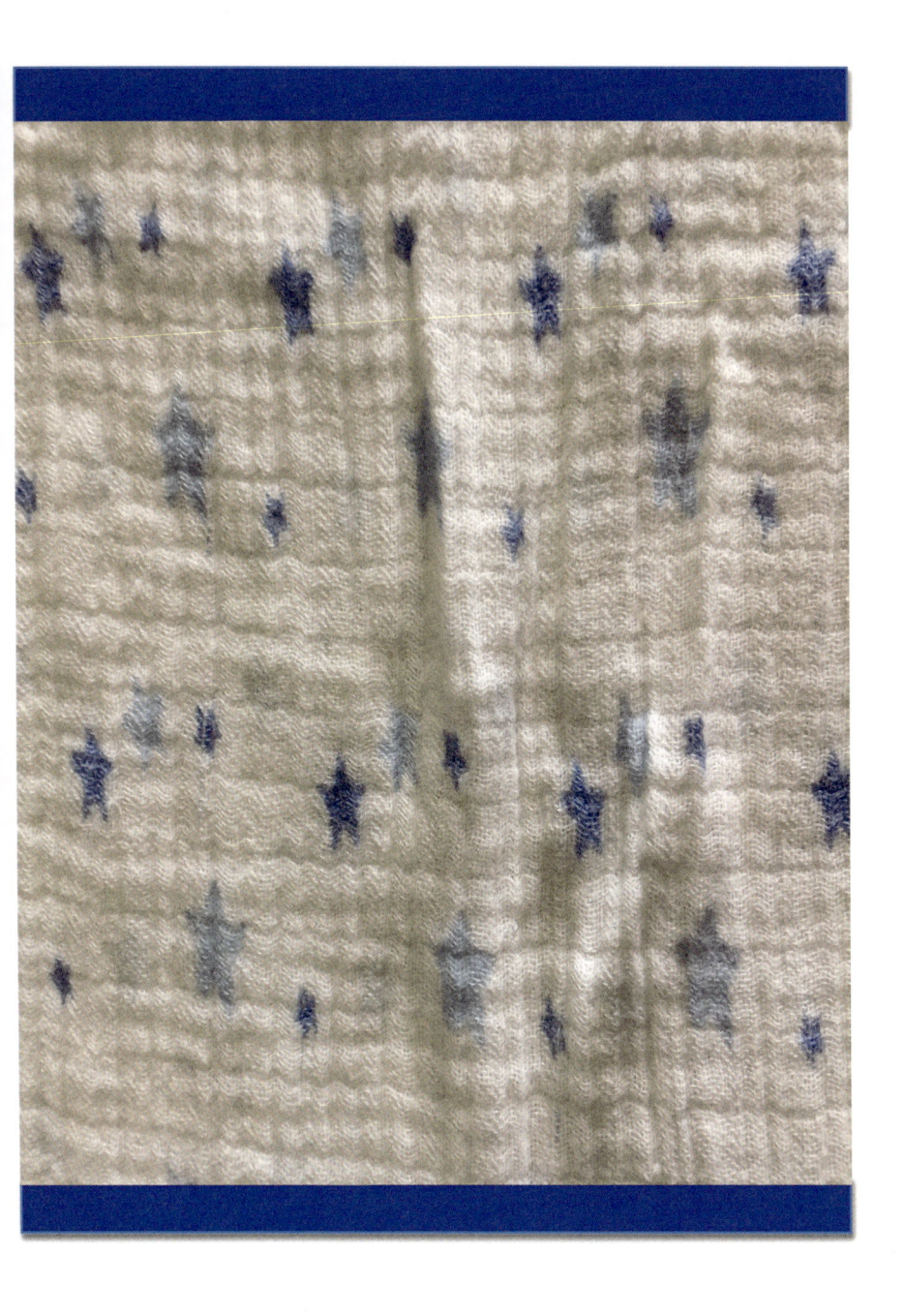

Made in the USA
Columbia, SC
17 November 2018